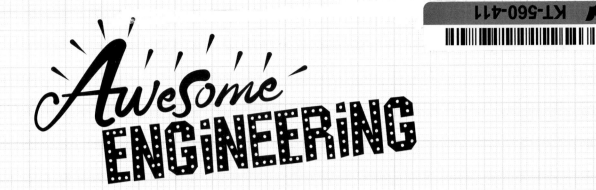

SKYSCRAPERS

SALLY SPRAY

WITH ARTWORK BY MARK RUFFLE

W

FRANKLIN WATTS

Franklin Watts

Published in paperback in Great Britain in 2019
by The Watts Publishing Group
Copyright © The Watts Publishing Group, 2017

Series editor: Paul Rockett
Series design and illustration: Mark Ruffle
www.rufflebrothers.com
Consultant:
Andrew Woodward BEng (Hons) CEng MICE FCIArb

ISBN 978 1 4451 5526 5

Printed in Dubai

Franklin Watts
An imprint of
Hachette Children's Group
Part of The Watts Publishing Group
Carmelite House
50 Victoria Embankment
London EC4Y 0DZ
An Hachette UK Company
www.hachette.co.uk
www.franklinwatts.co.uk

CONTENTS

BUILD IT TALL

Skyscrapers shape our city skylines; they reach jaw-dropping heights and create unusual and wondrous shapes. Building tall and inspiring skyscrapers all over the world requires ambition, imagination and engineering genius.

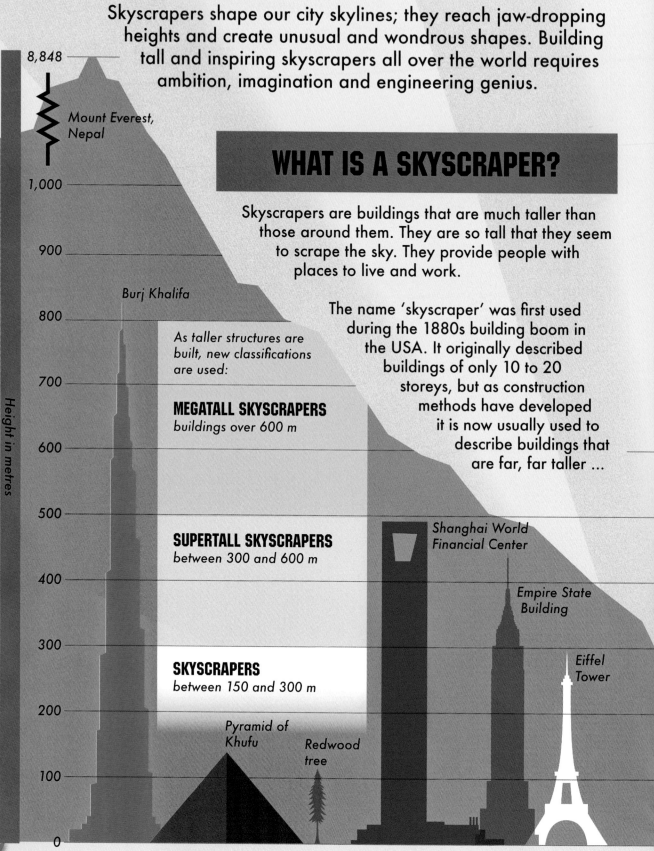

8,848

Mount Everest, Nepal

1,000

900

Burj Khalifa

800

700

600

500

400

300

200

Pyramid of Khufu

Redwood tree

100

0

Height in metres

WHAT IS A SKYSCRAPER?

Skyscrapers are buildings that are much taller than those around them. They are so tall that they seem to scrape the sky. They provide people with places to live and work.

The name 'skyscraper' was first used during the 1880s building boom in the USA. It originally described buildings of only 10 to 20 storeys, but as construction methods have developed it is now usually used to describe buildings that are far, far taller ...

As taller structures are built, new classifications are used:

MEGATALL SKYSCRAPERS
buildings over 600 m

SUPERTALL SKYSCRAPERS
between 300 and 600 m

SKYSCRAPERS
between 150 and 300 m

Shanghai World Financial Center

Empire State Building

Eiffel Tower

4

WHY BUILD A SKYSCRAPER?

Since ancient times people have built tall structures to show off their wealth and power. Pyramids, cathedrals and mosques were built to be large and visible. Skyscrapers really took off in 1930s' New York, when large companies competed to build the tallest skyscraper in the world.

The practical reason for building upwards is to save on ground space. This has become even more important as cities grow and more space is needed to house people and offices.

Skyscrapers in New York

SKYSCRAPER CHALLENGES

Building high brings many challenges. Skyscrapers must be strong enough to support their own weight, plus the live load (the people and things inside them), and sturdy enough to withstand wild weather and even earthquakes.

To ensure a successful and innovative skyscraper, teams of engineers, architects and surveyors need to carefully consider the building brief, plan the design, and choose the correct materials and techniques for the job.

Clever engineering means the sky's the limit for skyscrapers!

The Tokyo Skytree is the tallest structure in the world, but it has no offices or homes so it's not a skyscraper.

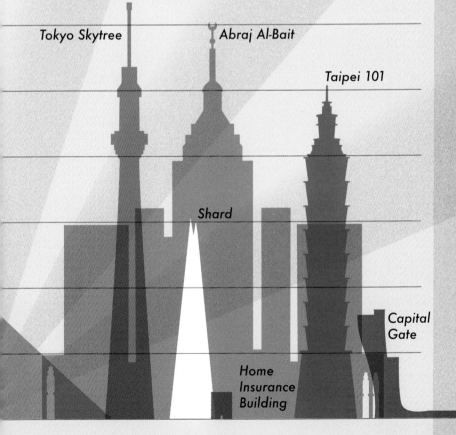

Tokyo Skytree

Abraj Al-Bait

Taipei 101

Shard

Capital Gate

Home Insurance Building

HOME INSURANCE BUILDING

Built in 1885 in Chicago, USA, the Home Insurance Building is considered to be the first skyscraper in the world. It revolutionised the way buildings were designed and made, introducing strong materials and sparking future ambitions to build high.

BUILDING BRIEF

Build an office building that makes maximum use of the limited ground space available in Chicago.

Architect: William Le Baron Jenney

Location: Chicago, USA

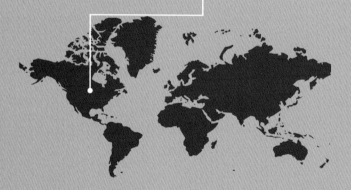

By today's standards, the Home Insurance Building was not tall. It was demolished in 1931 to make way for a taller skyscraper, the Field Building.

METAL FRAME

The height of the Home Insurance Building was achieved by using a metal frame as a skeleton structure. Architect William Jenney got the idea for building a metal frame after seeing his wife put a large, heavy book on top of a wire birdcage, and it supported the weight of the book easily. Jenney realised that the weight was spread evenly through the thin wires of the cage making the structure more balanced.

STEEL STRENGTH

At the start of the building process, cast and wrought iron were used for the skeleton frame. Partway through, Jenney decided to try a new metal – steel. Using steel was such a new idea that worried city officials stopped the construction to assess the safety of the building.

Jenney was right to use steel as it is a much better building material than iron; it's lighter, harder and does not rust as easily. His clever engineering changed the way future skyscrapers would be built – with supporting steel frames.

As the steel frame rather than brick walls was supporting the building, the Home Insurance Building could have lots of large windows to light the interior.

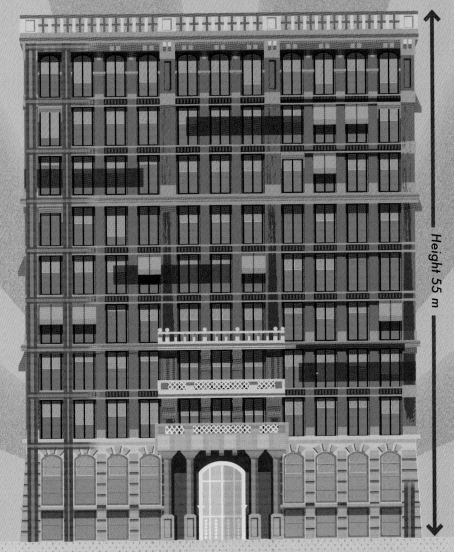

Height 55 m

PYRAMID FOUNDATIONS

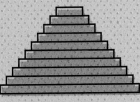

Several pyramid-shaped foundations were used. These were six-metre-deep and made from layers of stone, concrete and rubble.

Gravity is a constant downward force and as each storey is added to a building the weight increases. To support this weight there has to be a sturdy base, usually built underground, known as the foundations. The Home Insurance Building had pyramid-shaped foundations. With the widest area at the bottom and smaller squares on top, this shape helped to balance and hold the weight of the building above. This is called a spread footing (see page 9).

CHRYSLER BUILDING

In the early 1930s New York experienced a building boom with skyscrapers popping up all over the city. It was an era of new machinery and technological development, reflected in the iconic design of the Chrysler Building.

Height 319 m

BUILDING BRIEF

Build the tallest and most impressive building in the world. It should work as a landmark and an office space for the Chrysler car company.

Architect: William Van Alen

Location: New York City, USA

RACE FOR THE SKY

The car manufacturer Walter Chrysler wanted a building that was taller and grander than any other in the world. To ensure it was the tallest, the architect added a surprise, a 38 m spire assembled in secret in the lift shaft. This made the Chrysler Building the tallest building in the world in 1930, but just 11 months later it was overtaken by the Empire State Building, built just a few blocks away.

The building was designed to reflect the style of Chrysler's cars: the eagle head ornaments and the tower's curves match those on the cars that were displayed in the ground floor showroom.

STEEL SKELETON

The Chrysler Building is constructed around a rigid steel frame. Vertical steel columns, sitting on underground foundations, support the weight of the building. Horizontal beams attached to the vertical columns support the weight of the roof and each storey. The columns and beams were secured using metal pins, called rivets.

The steel frame, not the surrounding bricks, holds the building up. The brick covering is called a curtain wall. It is attached to the frame and provides decorative weatherproofing, but not structural support.

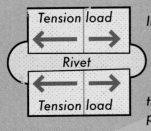

In total, 391,881 rivets were used to bolt the frame of the Chrysler Building together. Rivets are good at supporting tension loads, firmly holding the beams that are trying to pull apart.

EXTERIOR DESIGN

The building is a beautiful example of Art Deco design – a new, modern style that was popular in the 1920s and 1930s. The white brick exterior makes it appear light and bright. The tower is made up of seven overlapping arches that narrow towards the top creating an illusion of perspective, making the building look even taller than it is. The tower is clad in a shimmering steel, new at the time, called 'Enduro KA-2'. It was tested in rain and wind for months before being used. It has not tarnished, and has never been replaced.

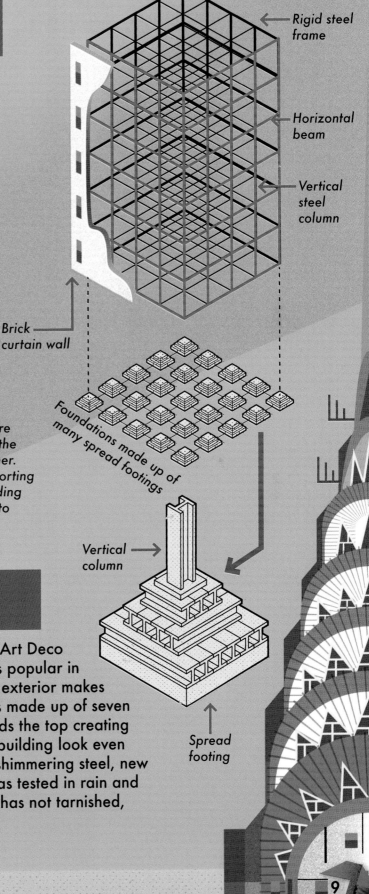

Rigid steel frame

Horizontal beam

Vertical steel column

Brick curtain wall

Foundations made up of many spread footings

Vertical column

Spread footing

EMPIRE STATE BUILDING

Completed in 1931, the Empire State Building is 443 m tall. It is an iconic landmark of the New York skyline and one of the most famous buildings in the world.

BUILDING BRIEF

Build the tallest building in New York and the world – beat the Chrysler Building. Design so that sunlight can still reach the streets below.

Architects:
Shreve, Lamb and Harmon

Structural engineer:
Homer G Balcom

Location: New York City, USA

Height 443 m

EFFICIENT BUILDING

The design and construction process for the Empire State Building was incredibly efficient. The architectural drawings took only two weeks to be completed and the building process ran on a strict schedule with a construction rate of four-and-a-half storeys a week.

It was built at a time of change in the building industry. New ways of working were introduced, such as assembly lines, delivering pieces on specially laid rail tracks, and having chutes that allowed the bricks to be dropped and hoisted around the site. This made things speedy, reducing the use of workers pushing wheelbarrows, and kept the surrounding area clear of building materials.

ELEVATORS

The rise of skyscrapers would not have been possible without the invention of the safety elevator, in 1853. No one wants to live or work in a hundred-storey building where stairs are the only way to get to the top! The Empire State Building has elevators in its centre surrounded by a steel support frame. This adds further stability to the skyscraper's inner core.

When it opened the Empire State Building had 64 elevators. Today it has 73.

Steel supports around the elevators

A worker with a head for heights fixes a beam in place.

Original floor plan of the 58th floor

HEIGHT

As more skyscrapers were built, New York City introduced a law requiring tall buildings to taper as they went up, allowing sunlight to reach the city streets below. This can be seen in the Empire State Building's design – it decreases in size as it rises to the apex (the top). The staggered shape of the building also has a structural advantage, as the larger sections below support the smaller sections above.

The Empire State Building has been seen in around 200 films, most famously being climbed by the giant gorilla in the King Kong films made in 1933 and 2005.

Staggered apex

The mast at the top of the Empire State Building was designed as a place to tether airships. In practice this proved too dangerous, as strong winds running up the sides of the building caused the airships to blow, around making them highly unstable.

11

WILLIS TOWER

Originally known as the Sears Tower, the Willis Tower was completed in 1973 using a new way of grouping steel frames together. This revolutionised skyscraper design and allowed buildings to be taller, stronger, cheaper, as well as more architecturally interesting.

BUILDING BRIEF

Use a new and innovative design to construct an office building to house the headquarters of the biggest retailer in the world.

Architect: Bruce Graham at Skidmore, Owings and Merrill

Structural engineer: Fazlur Rahman Khan

Location: Chicago, USA

BUNDLED TUBE STRUCTURE

Engineer Fazlur Khan came up with a new way to construct skyscrapers using a bundled tube structure system. This places multiple steel frames alongside each other. Clustered together they provide greater strength and resistance to wind, earthquakes and stress from the upper weight of the building. The Willis Tower uses a bundle of nine steel frames.

> 'When thinking design, I put myself in the place of a whole building, feeling every part. In my mind I visualise the stresses and twisting a building undergoes.'
>
> Fazlur Khan, Engineer

Bundled tube structure and floor plan

Placing smaller frames around the outside supports the weight of the tallest frames

CANTILEVER

The bundled tube structure uses the smaller tube frames around the outside to act as a support for the taller frames. They resist the sideways and downwards loads of the taller frames and distribute the weight through the building. This is called a cantilever, when a section can successfully extend outwards or upwards because it is well supported by the main structure. It's like a giant diving board, held in place at one end.

Skydeck

Height 520 m

Tallest in the world from 1973 to 1998

Storeys 91–108

Storeys 67–90

Storeys 51–66

Storeys 1–50

SKYDECK

The Skydeck was added to the tower in 1974. It is formed from retractable glass boxes, 412 m above the ground. They are held in place on steel cantilevers fixed into the side of the building. The boxes can move out from the face of the building on rails.

← 1.3m →

The boxes are supported on steel cantilever rails hidden inside the building.

Each Skydeck box is made from three layers of 1.2-cm-thick glass, with a strong thin steel frame at the edge. It gives the occupants the impression of being suspended in air.

13

PETRONAS TWIN TOWERS

At 452 m in height, the Petronas Twin Towers form the tallest twin-tower skyscraper in the world. They were designed to be the focus of the skyline in Kuala Lumpur, the capital city of Malaysia. Engineers had to contend with the soft soil and strong winds during the planning and construction.

BUILDING BRIEF

Build a twin-towered skyscraper to house businesses and shops. It should reflect the cultural heritage of Malaysia and Islamic architectural style. It must be able to withstand wind speeds of 100 km/h.

Architect: César Pelli

Structural engineer: Thornton Tomasetti

Location: Kuala Lumpur, Malaysia

MOVING BRIDGE

The two towers are connected on the 41st and 42nd floors by a bridge, known as the Skybridge. The bridge is constructed so that it is not fixed to either tower, but can slide in and out. High winds cause the towers to sway and move away from each other by up to 75 cm. If the Skybridge was fixed in place winds would easily damage it.

The Skybridge is supported underneath by a triangular arch. This flexes on spherical bearings, allowing movement and working in a similar way to the human hip joint.

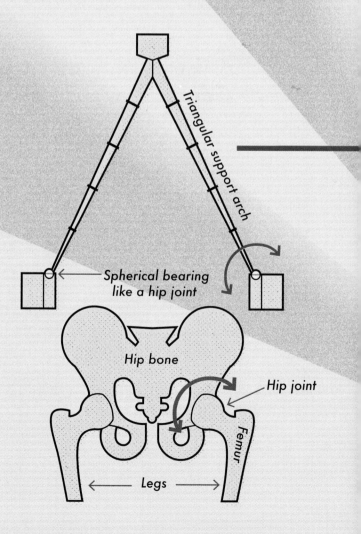

Triangular support arch

Spherical bearing like a hip joint

Hip bone

Hip joint

Femur

Legs

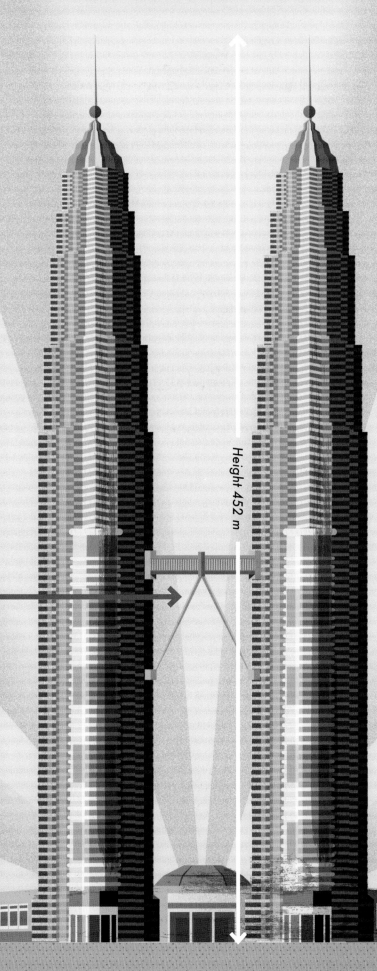

Height 452 m

FOUNDATIONS

Early in development it was discovered that the ground was too soft to support the towers' weight. So the engineers and designers had to build really deep foundations, digging down until they hit strong limestone rock. They filled the space between the surface and the limestone with 104 concrete piles of varying lengths for each tower. The shortest pile was 60 m in length and the longest was 114 m.

CONCRETE

The towers are built using concrete with steel rods running through it, known as reinforced concrete. This was cheaper than using a steel frame as less steel needed to be imported. Reinforced concrete is more rigid, so it is better at reducing a building's sway. However, it does make the finished building much heavier – not so much a problem when you have the world's deepest foundations.

Steel rods →

Concrete →

Reinforced concrete

30 ST MARY AXE

The skyline of London is filled with many unusual-shaped skyscrapers, such as 30 St Mary Axe. Also known as the Gherkin, due to its cylindrical shape, its eye-catching design fulfils the practical needs of the space both inside and outside of the building.

BUILDING BRIEF

Build an energy-saving office building in the financial district of London. It needs to fit within the exact space of the previous building on that site and have a new and exciting design.

Architects: Norman Foster and Ken Shuttleworth

Structural engineer: Arup

Location: London, UK

Height 180 m

A DIAGRID

30 St Mary Axe has a supporting steel framework called a diagrid. The steel framework is made from diagonally intersecting ribs of steel that are welded or bolted together.

The diagrid supports the weight of the building, distributing the loads in a downwards zig-zag pattern through the diagonal beams. This removes the need for vertical columns inside, allowing for more space and light throughout the building.

'[Diagrid is] a series of triangles that combine gravity and lateral support into one, making the building stiff, efficient and lighter than a traditional high-rise.'

Cantor Seinuk, Structural engineer

COMPUTER DESIGN

Early plans of the building were tested on a computer using a modelling software usually used in the design of aeroplanes and space rockets. The tests revealed that flat panes of glass could be used, rather than pieces of curved glass. In fact, curved glass is only used right at the top of the building.

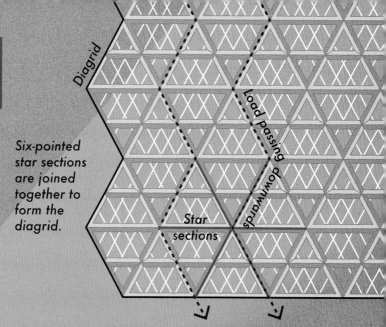

Six-pointed star sections are joined together to form the diagrid.

Diagrid

Load passing downwards

Star sections

The diagrid can be seen in the diamond and triangular patterns on the building's exterior.

ENERGY EFFICIENT

The weather and the use of computers have created a heating system that uses half the energy of other skyscrapers this size. Air blowing against the exterior of the building is allowed in through gaps in the walls. Once inside, the air is warmed through the external glass – this is known as 'solar gain'. A computer system constantly monitors the temperature of the building and opens the windows when it gets too hot.

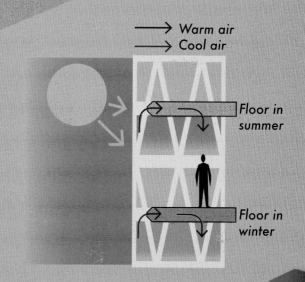

→ Warm air
→ Cool air

Floor in summer

Floor in winter

TAIPEI 101

At 509 m, Taipei 101 is one of the tallest skyscrapers in the world. It stands in Taiwan's capital city, Taipei, just 200 m from a major fault line – an area of earthquake activity.

BUILDING BRIEF

Build a landmark iconic skyscraper that can withstand typhoon winds and earthquakes.

Architects: C Y Lee & Partners

Structural engineer: Thornton Tomasetti

Location: Taipei, Taiwan

GIANT PENDULUM

Taipei 101 has an unusual engineering feature that hangs between its 88th and 92nd floors: a large steel sphere, called a 'tuned mass damper' (TMD). This acts as a giant pendulum, moving slightly back and forth, to reduce any movement of the building.

When an earthquake strikes, the TMD swings in the same direction as the sway of the building but with a time lag. This reduces the amount of sway.

The foundations are built 80 m deep into the ground.

In 1999, an earthquake in Taipei destroyed over 10,000 buildings.

This skyscraper is named after its home city and the number of floors it has above ground: 101.

Taipei 101's TMD is the largest in the world. It is 5.5 m in diameter and weighs 662 tonnes.

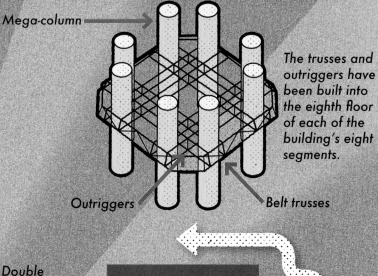

Height 509 m

MEGA-COLUMNS

Taipei 101's exterior has eight mega-columns. These are steel columns packed with super-strength concrete. The mega-columns are connected to each other with belt trusses and to internal steel columns with outriggers. These are beams that reach across a structure, helping to stabilise its frame.

Mega-column

The trusses and outriggers have been built into the eighth floor of each of the building's eight segments.

Outriggers

Belt trusses

Double notch corners

CORNERS

The corners on each section are designed to minimise the impact of strong winds. They feature a double notch design that breaks up the wind's force as it hits and moves around the building.

WIND

BAHRAIN WORLD TRADE CENTER

Built in 2008, the Bahrain World Trade Center is the world's first wind-powered skyscraper. The 240-m-tall twin towers are linked by three bridges, each supporting a giant wind turbine.

BUILDING BRIEF

Build a new trade centre to add a focal point to a revitalised part of Manama city. Give some thought to the sustainability and green credentials of the building.

Architect: Shaun Killa at Atkins

Structural engineer: Atkins

Location: Manama, Bahrain

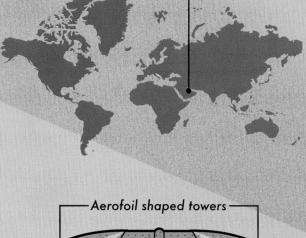

Manama skyline from the sea with the towering Bahrain World Trade Center

AEROFOIL SAILS

Built right next to the sea, the building looks like an enormous sailing ship. However the design is more than just decorative; the shape of the towers helps to power the wind turbines that sit between them.

From overhead, each tower appears eliptical, like the aerofoil shape of an aeroplane wing. This helps to funnel air coming in from the sea between the two curved towers straight towards the turbines.

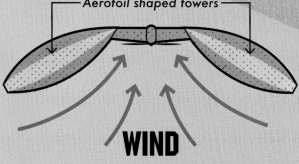

Aerofoil shaped towers

WIND

Overhead view of Bahrain World Trade Center

WIND POWER

Buildings consume a third of the world's energy and so it's important that they become more energy-efficient. Architect Shaun Killa designed the Bahrain WTC to have a self-generating power source – the wind turbines. Each turbine is 29 m in diameter, and as they turn they produce 11–15 per cent of the power needed for the whole building.

Height 240 m

HOW THEY WORK

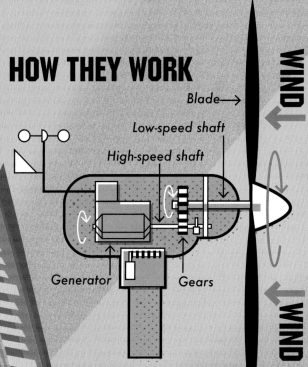

WIND

Blade→

Low-speed shaft

High-speed shaft

Generator

Gears

WIND

Wind turbines transform some of the kinetic energy from the wind into electrical power. The wind turns the blades of the turbine, which rotate a rod connected to a generator. The spin is increased in the generator and electric power is produced.

BURJ KHALIFA

In 2009 the Burj Khalifa became the tallest building in the world. At 830 m high, it belongs to a growing number of megatall skyscrapers. It's an impressive landmark and a hard-to-miss sight in Dubai, one of the planet's fastest growing cities.

BUILDING BRIEF

Build a centrepiece for Downtown Dubai, an expanding area of homes and hotels. Make it impressive to attract visitors and businesses to the country.

Architect: Adrian Smith at Skidmore, Owings and Merrill

Structural engineer: Bill Baker

Location: Dubai, UAE

Height 850 m

BUTTRESSED CORE

Burj Khalifa uses a bundled tube structure (see page 12), and has a hexagonal frame at the centre of the building, called the buttressed core. This acts like a mega-strong spine supporting the building as it rises. The buttressed core is supported at ground level by three outward sections.

As the building rises, the tower tapers in 27 different places to form an ascending spiral, a complex but sturdy design. The buttressed core emerges from the top of the building like a giant minaret tower on a mosque.

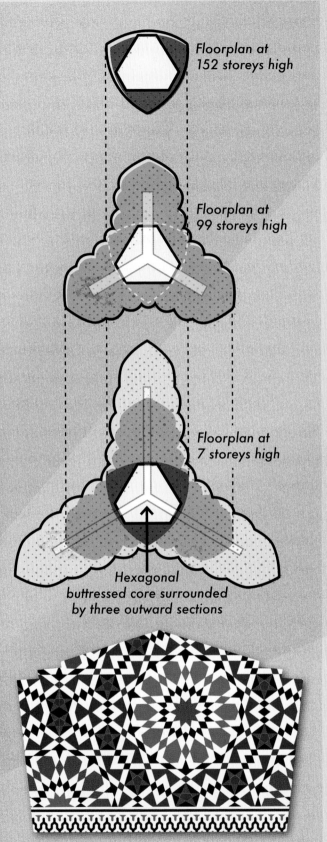

Floorplan at 152 storeys high

Floorplan at 99 storeys high

Floorplan at 7 storeys high

Hexagonal buttressed core surrounded by three outward sections

The design for the floor plan incorporates traditional pentagon and triangle patterns typical of the Islamic style.

CONFUSING THE WIND

With its tapering and jagged sides, the design of the Burj Khalifa reduces the strength of the wind. When wind hits the exterior it is deflected at different speeds and directions and loses some of its power to damage the building. The exterior design went through 40 different tests in wind tunnels to ensure it would stand up well to strong wind forces.

This diagram shows how the design of the building at different heights deflects the wind in various ways.

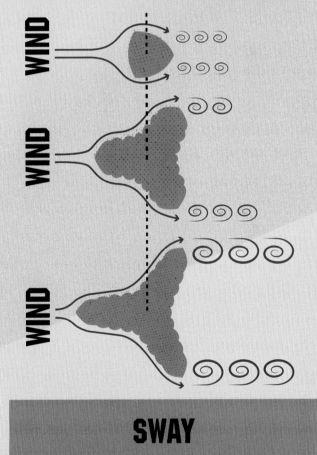

WIND

WIND

WIND

SWAY

The Burj Khalifa can sway 1.5 m at the top. This may sound dramatic, but the structure has to give a little with the wind. If it was engineered to not move and be totally rigid it would put too much stress on the whole building and risk it all falling over. Buildings have to sway, a bit like branches on a tree.

BOSCO VERTICALE

Italian for 'vertical forest', Bosco Verticale is the name of a pair of eco-friendly buildings built in 2014 in Milan, Italy. They may not be supertall skyscrapers, but they are super-innovative, merging structural and landscape design so that high-rise living doesn't mean living without a garden.

BUILDING BRIEF

Build a residential block for the busy city of Milan. It should promote sustainability and biodiversity and reduce air, heat and noise pollution for the residents.

Architects: Stefano Boeri, Gianandrea Barreca, Giovanni La Varra at Boeri Studio

Location: Milan, Italy

Tower one

Tower two

Height 112 m

Height 80 m

URBAN FOREST

Architect Stefano Boeri wanted the Bosco Verticale to have a living façade that would change and grow over the seasons. He talked with botanists for two years to plan which plants would thrive above the city, coming up with over 90 different species. The balconies on the 26 floors of tower one and 18 floors of tower two are home to over 730 trees, 5,000 shrubs and 11,000 perennial (long-lasting) plants – enough for a small forest!

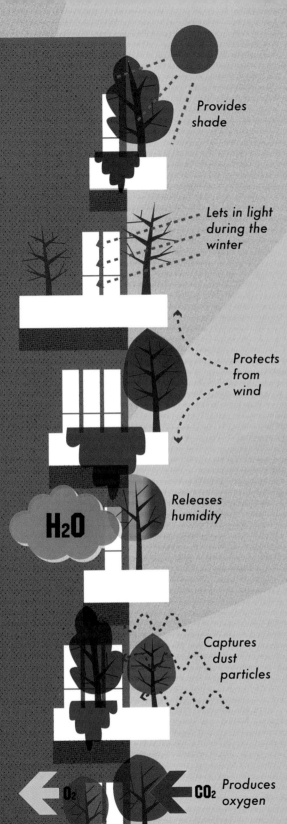

Provides shade

Lets in light during the winter

Protects from wind

H_2O

Releases humidity

Captures dust particles

O_2 CO_2 *Produces oxygen*

Reduces noise pollution

BIOCLIMATIC

The towers were built to be 'bioclimatic'. Bioclimatic architecture connects directly with nature, taking into account the climate and environmental conditions of its location. The green screen planting on the Bosco Veticale helps to cut down on air pollution by absorbing carbon monoxide. It also reduces the noise from the busy streets, filters dust, and helps to regulate the temperature inside, keeping it warmer in winter and cooler in summer.

The design provides a lovely garden view for the occupants, and helps to soften the hard edges of the exterior.

HEAVY SUPPORT

Reinforced concrete beams are used throughout, which make the buildings very heavy, but also very strong – essential for supporting the weight of the plants that live there, and for the soil they need. The balconies are a cantilever design, with the supported end secured in the building. They extend 3.3 m outwards, with trees planted at the edge and tied into place so that they don't fall and damage the building or the street below.

SHANGHAI TOWER

At 632 m, the Shanghai Tower is one of the tallest buildings in the world. Completed in 2015, its twisting cutting-edge design helps make it one of the most sustainable supertowers and a landmark design for future skyscrapers.

The Shanghai Tower (right) completes a trio of skyscrapers in the city's financial district. It stands alongside the Jin Mao Tower (centre) and the Shanghai World Financial Center (left).

BUILDING BRIEF

Design an eco-friendly building to provide lots of office space, plus community areas for people to enjoy.

Architects: Daniel Winey, Jun Xia and Marshall Strabala at Gensler

Structural engineers: Thornton Tomasetti

Location: Shanghai, China

Height 632 m

GREEN POWER

The Shanghai Tower has been described as 'the greenest super high-rise building on earth'. Its energy needs are supplied from different sources, including wind turbines, solar panels and geothermal energy (heat taken from the ground). Horizontal wind turbines are located 580 m up in the side curve of the building. The wind speed is fast up here and drives the turbines to produce enough electrical energy to light the whole building.

WIND

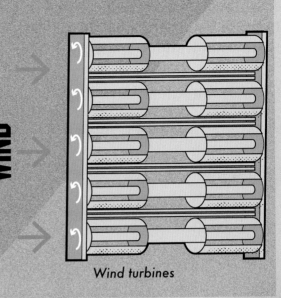

Wind turbines

External glass curtain wall

Internal glass curtain wall

There are nine areas inbetween the glass walls that contain public spaces and sky gardens.

GLASS

The Shanghai Tower is built with two glass curtain walls that help to control the internal temperature. The space inbetween the glass warms the cool air in winter and reduces the heat in summer, making it very energy efficient.

Most skyscrapers use tinted, reflective glass that is designed to lower the absorption of heat. The success of the Shanghai Tower's double glass layer design meant that it could be built with transparent glass. This allows people to see in and out of the building and lets more light inside.

TWISTING SHAPE

The façade's unique cylindrical shape turns and tapers towards the top. This design reduces the wind load hitting the tower by 24 per cent and it can even withstand typhoons.

'This building is about China's future, which is more transparent, more open – it's a building for people.'

Marshall Strabala, Architect

FASCINATING FACTS

Skyscrapers come in many weird and wonderful forms. Here is a collection of awesome skyscraper facts from all around the world.

Hong Kong is the city that has the most skyscrapers in the world. The highest of all is the **International Commerce Centre**, completed in 2010, standing 484 m tall.

It's all very well building massively tall glass skyscrapers, but how on earth do you clean the windows? Each of the **Petronas Twin Towers** *has around 16,000 panes of glass; cleaning cars extend out of hidden compartments at the top of buildings. It takes two months to clean both towers and the cleaners need a head for heights!*

At nearly 310 m tall, the **Shard** in London is one of Europe's tallest buildings. The exterior looks like shards of glass balanced against each other, hence its name. The shimmering exterior is made up of 11,000 glass panels, and an amazing 95 per cent of the materials used to build it are recycled.

Home Insurance Building

The Elephant Building

Bosco Verticale

Guangzhou Circle

30 St Mary Axe

The Turning Torso

Bahrain World Trade Center

The Shard

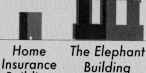

STRANGE SHAPES

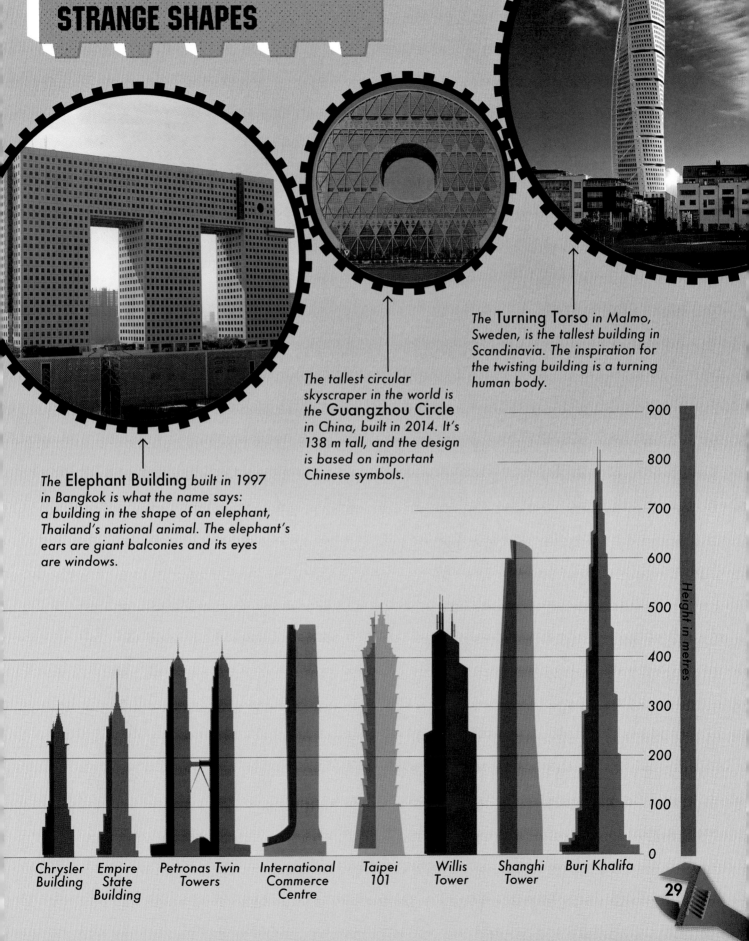

The **Elephant Building** built in 1997 in Bangkok is what the name says: a building in the shape of an elephant, Thailand's national animal. The elephant's ears are giant balconies and its eyes are windows.

The tallest circular skyscraper in the world is the **Guangzhou Circle** in China, built in 2014. It's 138 m tall, and the design is based on important Chinese symbols.

The **Turning Torso** in Malmo, Sweden, is the tallest building in Scandinavia. The inspiration for the twisting building is a turning human body.

Height in metres

900
800
700
600
500
400
300
200
100
0

Chrysler Building

Empire State Building

Petronas Twin Towers

International Commerce Centre

Taipei 101

Willis Tower

Shanghi Tower

Burj Khalifa

FURTHER INFORMATION

BOOKS

Amazing Jobs: Engineering by Colin Hyson (Wayland, 2016)

Bizarre Buildings by Anne Rooney (Franklin Watts, 2014)

Buildings, Bridges and Tunnels: An Accidental History of Inventions By Jon Richards (Franklin Watts, 2016)

A History of Britain in 12 Feats of Engineering by Paul Rockett (Franklin Watts, 2015)

Record-Breaking Buildings by Jon Richards and Ed Simkins (Franklin Watts, 2015)

WEBSITES

Information and engineering facts on skyscraper construction:
https://science.howstuffworks.com/engineering/structural/skyscraper.htm

Easy to understand information on the science of building skyscrapers:
www.explainthatstuff.com/howbuildingswork.html

Fun facts and information on some of the world's tallest buildings:
www.sciencekids.co.nz/sciencefacts/engineering/buildings.html

The CBBC website contains information, videos, news and facts about skyscrapers:
www.bbc.co.uk/cbbc/search?q=skyscrapers&sa_f=search-product

Every effort has been made by the Publishers to ensure that these websites are suitable for children, that they are of the highest educational value, and that they contain no inappropriate or offensive material. However, because of the nature of the Internet, it is impossible to guarantee that the contents of these sites will not be altered. We strongly advise that Internet access is supervised by a responsible adult.

GLOSSARY

aerofoil The curved shape of an object, often referring to the wings of a plane. Air flows faster over the top of an aerofoil shape and slower underneath it.

architect A person who designs and often supervises the construction of buildings.

Art Deco The design style of the 1920s and 1930s, featuring geometric shapes, curved lines and bold colour.

belt truss A framework that usually consists of rafters, posts and struts which ties together and supports a roof, bridge or other structure.

botanist A plant expert.

cantilever A long projecting beam or structure, fixed at one end.

carbon monoxide A gas released by cars that is poisonous to people.

concrete A building material made from mixing sand, cement, gravel and water together.

cultural heritage A broad term used to describe the traditions, beliefs, knowledge and way of life of a group of people, passed down from one generation to another.

curtain wall A wall that forms the outer layer of a building but does not support the roof or the building.

elliptical Oval-shaped.

engineer A person who designs, constructs and maintains buildings, machines and other structures.

fault lines A line visible on the surface of the earth which indicates that there is a boundary between one tectonic plate and another deep below.

force A push or a pull on an object.

foundations The load-bearing parts of a building or structure, often underground.

gear A wheel with teeth that slots together with others like it. A gear is used to transmit power from one part of a machine to another.

geothermal energy Energy (power) from the heat of the earth.

gravity A force of attraction between all objects. Earth's gravity makes objects fall to the ground and keeps us from floating off into space.

heritage A belonging or idea handed on from past generations.

horizontal Parallel to the ground or the horizon.

iconic Widely recognised, famous, outstanding.

innovative Advanced, new, inventive.

iron A hard metal extracted from iron ore, used in building, which rusts easily.

Islamic Relating to Islam, one of the world's major religions.

kinetic energy The energy an object has because it is moving.

limestone A hard rock used as a building material.

load The force that a structure is supporting or resisting.

outrigger A beam that projects beyond a wall to support an overhanging roof or extended floor.

perennial plants Plants that have a lifecycle of several years.

perimeter The outline or boundary.

reinforced concrete Concrete which has metal bars or wires contained within it.

rivet A metal pin capped on one end used for fixing metal plates together by hammering the uncapped end to secure.

spread footing A support for a column or wall that is larger than the thing it supports.

steel A strong, hard metal formed from iron, carbon and other materials.

storey Part of a building: all the rooms on one level.

stress Here, stress means the forces acting on a building or structure.

structural engineer A person who uses their skills to make sure that the design of a building and the materials used to build it will withstand the stresses and pressures put upon it.

surveyor In construction, a person who helps advise on whether a building is going to be safe and strong.

taper A gradual narrowing of an object or building.

tarnish Of materials, losing its shine.

tension load A pulling force.

turbines Machines that harness the energy from moving water, wind or gas and convert it into power.

urban A city or town environment.

vertical At right angles to the horizon or ground.

INDEX